This book is dedicated to my niece and her husband, Jacqui and Ian Kilpatrick, who share a love of the National Parks and encouraged us to visit Oregon.

A Close Up Look at

Crater Lake National Park

By Josie Zayac

Crater Lake is a park
With water so blue.
Come see for yourself-
A spectacular view.

Take a close look.
What is that?

It's called Wizard Island.
A sorcerer's hat.

Rising 700 feet high,
7,300 years old.
Wizard Island is a volcano
inside a volcano!

Take a close look.
What do you see?

The wind is so strong
It twists the tree.

Take a close look.
What do you see?

Gnarled
roots
from an
uprooted
tree.

Take a close look.
What do you see?

The berries of a whitebark
pine tree.

The wind is so strong
it bends all the trees.
The whitebark pine is
shaped like a "C".

Take a
close look.
What do
you see?

A castle
made
from a
volcano, how can that be?

Mount Mazama erupted.
Air and lava were warmed.
Lava flowed down the
mountain.
Pumice Castle was formed.

Take a close look.
What do you know?

Here we have pinnacles, formed by a volcano.

The river got buried due to volcanic explosion. Pinnacles were formed after years of erosion.

Take a close look.
What do you see?
It looks like a pirate ship-
lost at sea.

Phantom ship disappears as
the mist comes and goes.
It's rocks are the oldest-
over 400,000 years old.

Take a close look. What do you see?

Vidae Falls-
Where a river runs free.

Take a close look.
These flowers you'll adore.
Castle Crest Wildflower Trail-
Wildflowers galore.

Stroll through the meadow.
A river runs through it.

A peaceful
place.
Take your
parents to
it.

Crater Lake is the place with water so blue. It's a perfect example of what volcanoes can do.

You'll find castles and pirate ships with a bit of imagination. Crater Lake might be your next family vacation.

Facts about Crater Lake National Park, Oregon

- Established in 1902 as the sixth National Park
- Covers 183,000 acres
- Crater Lake is 1,943 feet deep, the deepest lake in the United States
- No rivers or streams feed the lake- only rain and snow- making it the cleanest large body of water in the world
- Mount Mazama is the volcano that collapsed to form Crater Lake 7,700 years ago

Look for other National Park books by Dr. Josie Zayac

- A Close Up Look at Bryce Canyon National Park
- A Close Up Look at Crater Lake National Park
- A Close Up Look at Cuyahoga Valley National Park
- A Close Up Look at Joshua Tree National Park
- A Close Up Look at Redwood National and State Parks
- A Close Up Look at Rocky Mountain National Park
- A Close Up Look at Sequoia National Park
- A Close Up Look at Theodore Roosevelt National Park
- A Close Up Look at Zion National Park

www.ingramcontent.com/pod-product-compliance
Lightning Source LLC
Chambersburg PA
CBHW050929290526
45792CB00002B/950